D0365183

Dear Parent:
Your child's love of reading starts here!

Every child learns to read in a different way and at his or her own speed. Some go back and forth between reading levels and read favorite books again and again. Others read through each level in order. You can help your young reader improve and become more confident by encouraging his or her own interests and abilities. From books your child reads with you to the first books he or she reads alone, there are I Can Read Books for every stage of reading:

My First

SHARED READING
Basic language, word repetition, and whimsical illustrations, ideal for sharing with your emergent reader

1

BEGINNING READING
Short sentences, familiar words, and simple concepts for children eager to read on their own

2

READING WITH HELP
Engaging stories, longer sentences, and language play for developing readers

3

READING ALONE
Complex plots, challenging vocabulary, and high-interest topics for the independent reader

4

ADVANCED READING
Short paragraphs, chapters, and exciting themes for the perfect bridge to chapter books

I Can Read Books have introduced children to the joy of reading since 1957. Featuring award-winning authors and illustrators and a fabulous cast of beloved characters, I Can Read Books set the standard for beginning readers.

A lifetime of discovery begins with the magical words **"I Can Read!"**

Visit www.icanread.com for information on enriching your child's reading experience.

m
a
E
B

I Can Read!™

READING 2 WITH HELP

Hamsters, Shells, and Spelling Bees School Poems

edited by
Lee Bennett Hopkins
pictures by Sachiko Yoshikawa

HarperCollins*Publishers*

Acknowledgments

Thanks are due to the following for use of works that appear in this collection:

Boyds Mills Press for "Not Fair" from *Somebody Catch My Homework* by David L. Harrison. Copyright © l993 by David L. Harrison. Reprinted by permission.

Curtis Brown, Ltd., for "Backpack Buddy" and "Ready" by Rebecca Kai Dotlich; copyright © 2008 by Rebecca Kai Dotlich. "My Teacher" by Lee Bennett Hopkins; copyright © 2008 by Lee Bennett Hopkins. "Maps" by Jane Yolen; copyright © 2008 by Jane Yolen. All reprinted by permission of Curtis Brown, Ltd.

Sandra Gilbert Brüg for "Listening." Used by permission of the author, who controls all rights.

Chetra Kotzas for "Lunch Bag." Used by permission of the author, who controls all rights.

Linda Kulp for "True Love." Used by permission of the author, who controls all rights.

J. Patrick Lewis for "Library" and "School Bus Driver." Used by permission of the author, who controls all rights.

Meadowbrook Press for "Measles" from *No More Homework! No More Tests!* by Bruce Lansky. Copyright © 1997 by Bruce Lansky. Reprinted with permission of Meadowbrook Press.

Leslie Danford Perkins for "Art Class." Used by permission of the author, who controls all rights.

Louis Phillips for "The Eraser Poem." Used by permission of the author, who controls all rights.

Heidi Bee Roemer for "Spelling Bee." Used by permission of the author, who controls all rights.

Alice Schertle for "Question." Used by permission of the author, who controls all rights.

Janet Settimo for "Hamster Math." Used by permission of the author, who controls all rights.

Ann Rousseau Smith for "Buzz." Used by permission of the author, who controls all rights.

Elizabeth Upton for "Show and Tell." Used by permission of the author, who controls all rights.

Amy Ludwig VanDerwater for "School Play." Used by permission of the author, who controls all rights.

Sharon Vargo for "Looking Through the Microscope." Used by permission of the author, who controls all rights.

HarperCollins®, ®, and I Can Read Book® are trademarks of HarperCollins Publishers.

Hamsters, Shells, and Spelling Bees: School Poems Text copyright © 2008 by Lee Bennett Hopkins Illustrations copyright © 2008 by Sachiko Yoshikawa All rights reserved. No part of this book may be used or reproduced in any manner whatsoever without written permission except in the case of brief quotations embodied in critical articles and reviews. Printed in the United States of America. For information address HarperCollins Children's Books, a division of HarperCollins Publishers, 1350 Avenue of the Americas, New York, NY 10019. www.harpercollinschildrens.com

Library of Congress Cataloging-in-Publication Data

Hopkins, Lee Bennett.

Hamsters, shells, and spelling bees : school poems / edited by Lee Bennett Hopkins ; pictures by Sachiko Yoshikawa.— 1st ed.

p. cm. — (An I can read book)

ISBN 978-0-06-074112-9 (trade bdg.)

ISBN 978-0-06-074113-6 (lib. bdg.)

I. Schools—Poetry. II. Title. III. Series.

PS595.S34 H36 2007 2007020881

811/.608—dc22 CIP

AC

1 2 3 4 5 6 7 8 9 10 ❖ First Edition

To my great-niece
Erin Elizabeth Bice
—L.B.H.

For Takako Hayakawa,
with special thanks to Namiko Rudi
—S.Y.

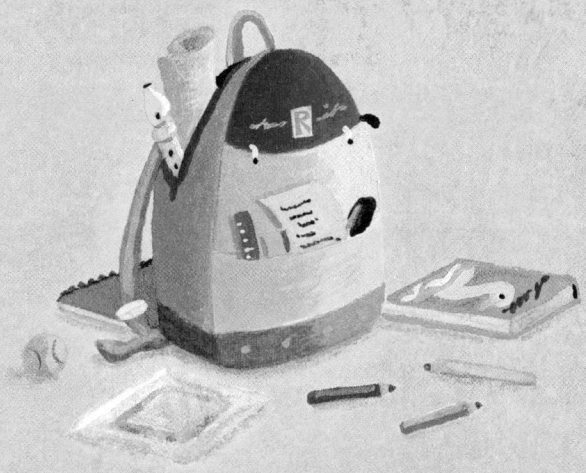

Contents

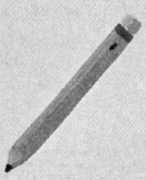

Ready by Rebecca Kai Dotlich 8

Hamster Math by Janet Settimo 10

School Bus Driver by J. Patrick Lewis 12

Backpack Buddy by Rebecca Kai Dotlich 14

My Teacher by Lee Bennett Hopkins 16

Show and Tell by Elizabeth Upton 18

Maps by Jane Yolen 20

Looking Through the Microscope by Sharon Vargo 22

Art Class by Leslie Danford Perkins 24

Library by J. Patrick Lewis 26

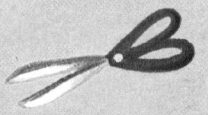

Listening by Sandra Gilbert Brüg 28

Lunch Bag by Chetra Kotzas 30

Buzz by Ann Rousseau Smith 32

Not Fair by David L. Harrison 34

Question by Alice Schertle 36

The Eraser Poem by Louis Phillips 38

Measles by Bruce Lansky 40

Spelling Bee by Heidi Bee Roemer 42

School Play by Amy Ludwig VanDerwater 44

True Love by Linda Kulp 46

IN·C
will
for

Ready

by Rebecca Kai Dotlich

Stars sleep as I wake

to this brand-new school day

ready

to

smile.

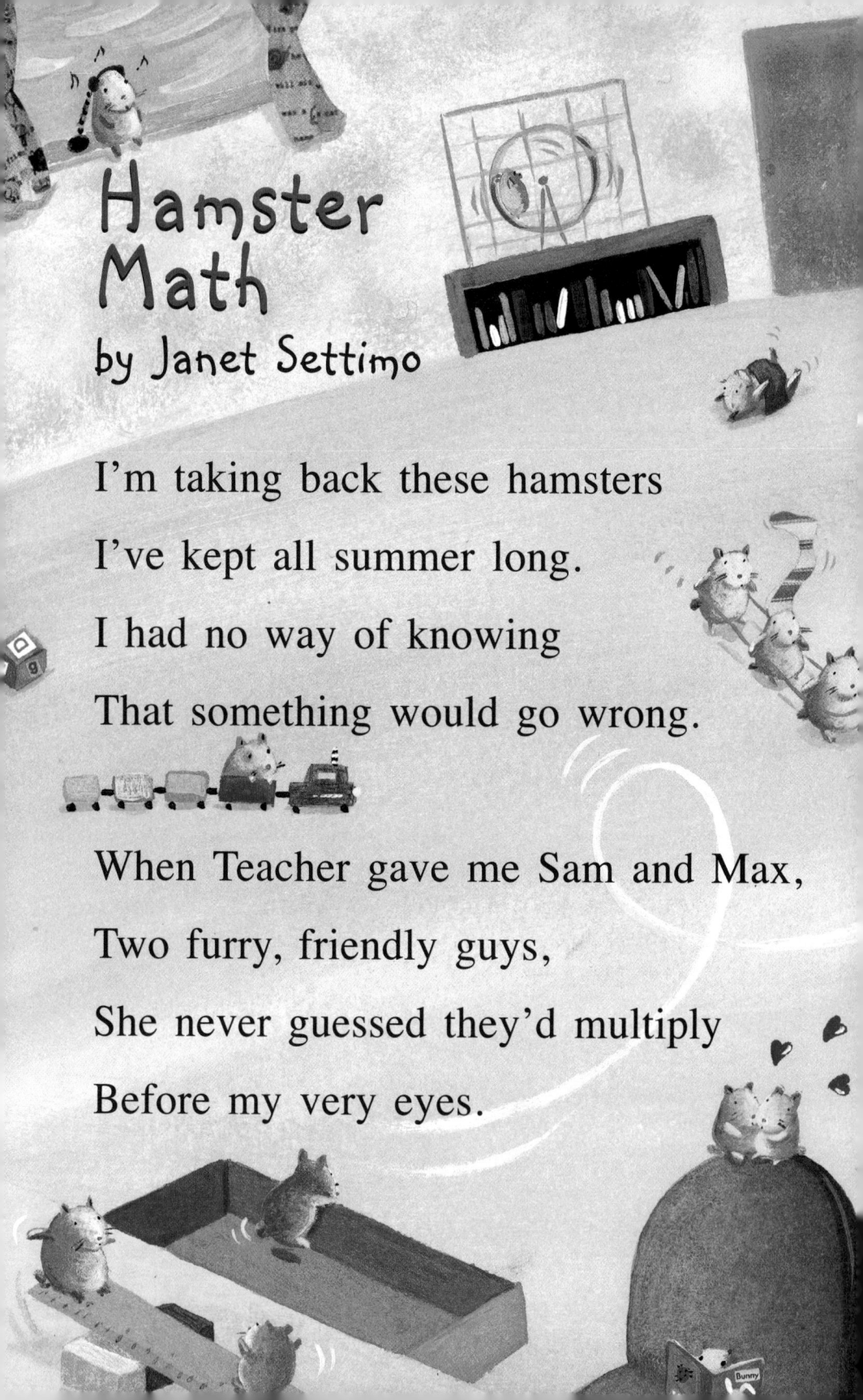

Hamster Math

by Janet Settimo

I'm taking back these hamsters
I've kept all summer long.
I had no way of knowing
That something would go wrong.

When Teacher gave me Sam and Max,
Two furry, friendly guys,
She never guessed they'd multiply
Before my very eyes.

I had hamsters on my dresser,
And hamsters in my drawer,
Hamsters on the windowsill,
And hamsters on the floor.

They were adding and dividing,
Multiplying by the score,
I never knew that one plus one
Could total twenty-four!

School Bus Driver

by J. Patrick Lewis

I hear the engine rumbling
As she sits out by the street,
Waiting for a slowpoke *(me!)*
To climb into his seat.

I don't know how she does it
Every day at 8:03,
Bur rain or snow or sleet I know
She's always there for me.

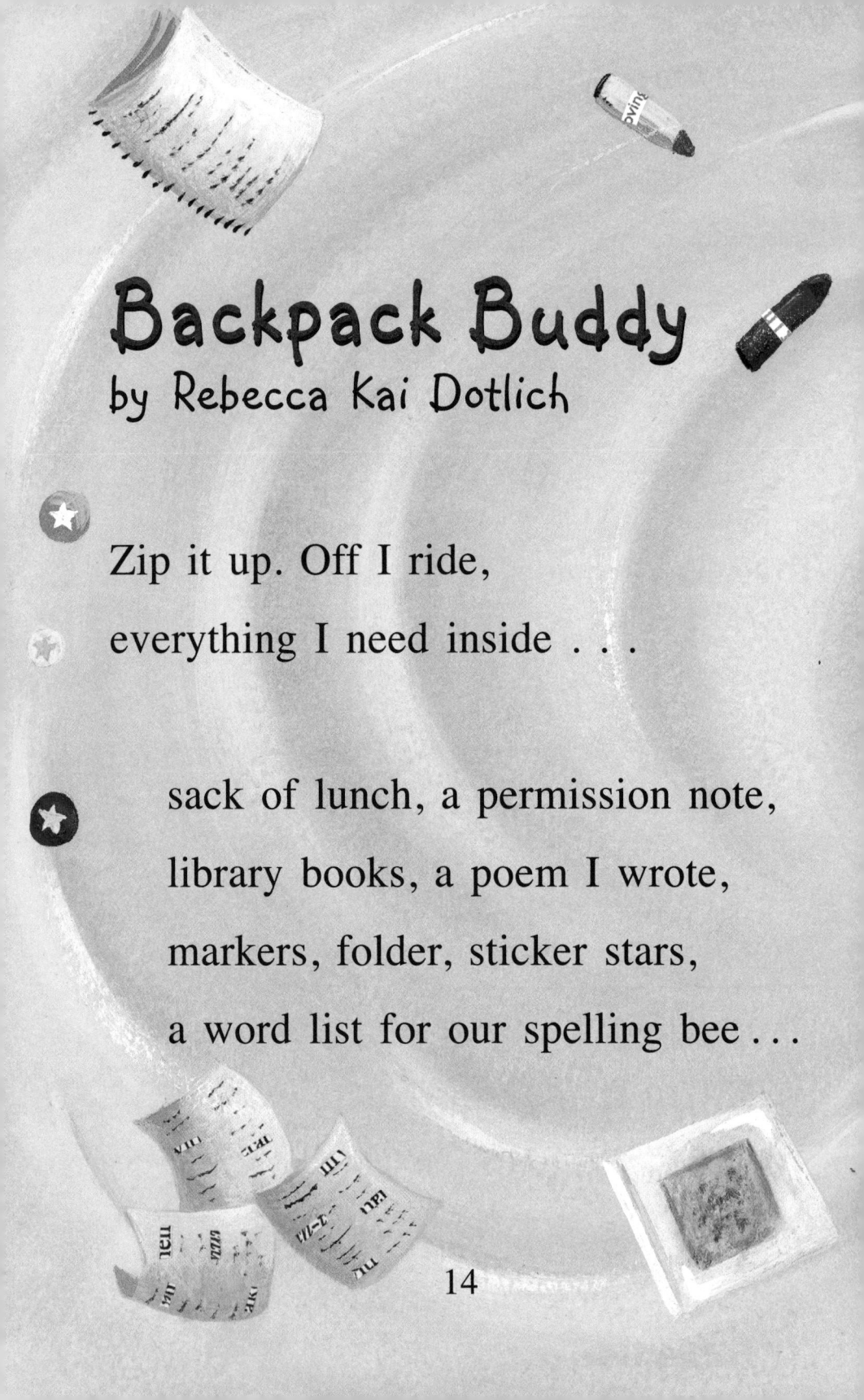

Backpack Buddy

by Rebecca Kai Dotlich

Zip it up. Off I ride,
everything I need inside . . .

sack of lunch, a permission note,
library books, a poem I wrote,
markers, folder, sticker stars,
a word list for our spelling bee . . .

Zip it up. Off I ride.

My backpack buddy and me.

My Teacher

by Lee Bennett Hopkins

My teacher
loves
reading books aloud
putting up new bulletin boards
taking vacations by the sea

but—

best of all
my teacher
loves
ME.

Show and Tell

by Elizabeth Upton

My shell
makes sounds
of waves rushing and crashing.
Somehow it saved up
seashore sounds
when it lived on the beach.
Do you want to hear
its ocean song?
Go ahead,
listen to my shell.

Maps

by Jane Yolen

We are making maps:
maps of our classroom,
maps of our school,
maps of our town.
We let our fingers walk
the straight lines
from window to door,
down school hallways
that gently curve,
along town streets
as crooked as question marks.

We trace old rail lines,
the bumps of mountains,
a blue swirl of river,
the broad turnpike lanes.
You can walk like that all day
and never get tired.

Looking Through the Microscope

by Sharon Vargo

I zoom in.
I zoom out.

Secret places
hidden spaces
captured by
a magic eye . . .

a tiny world
magnified.

Art Class

by Leslie Danford Perkins

Dream catchers hanging
with feathers and beads.
Pictures from popping corn,
lentils and seeds.

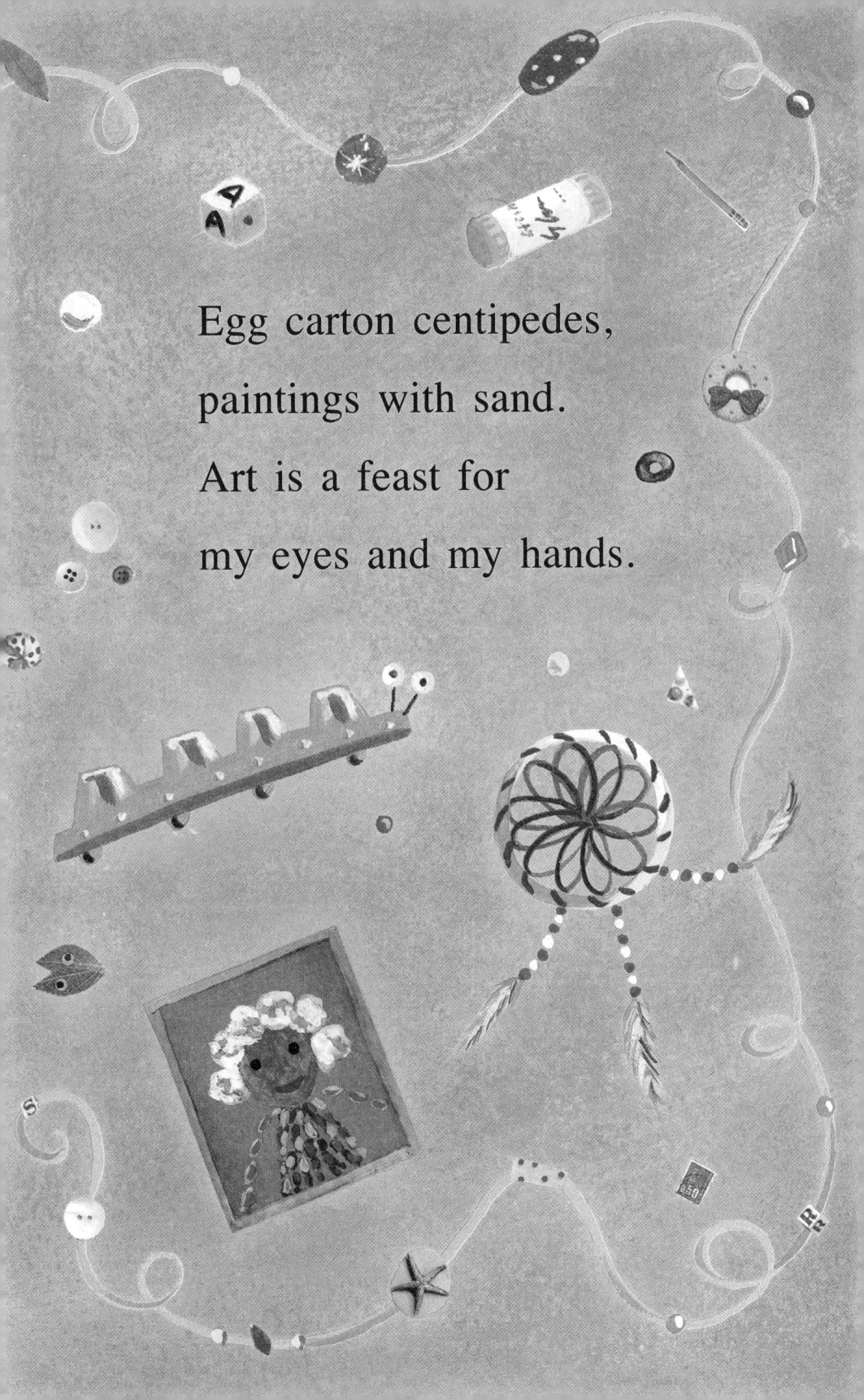

Egg carton centipedes,
paintings with sand.
Art is a feast for
my eyes and my hands.

Library

by J. Patrick Lewis

Come right in,
Look around
At all the treasures
That are bound
To make you glad
For a week or two
Until your treasure's
Overdue.

Listening

by Sandra Gilbert Brüg

I like to hear my teacher's voice
when she reads out loud
in our story nook.

Her voice
brings magical sounds
to each new character.

I sit close to my friends
on a fuzzy red rug—
like one big family

listening . . . loving
this book.

Pineapple

Lunch Bag

by Chetra Kotzas

Bulging
brown paper bag
hiding
one peanut butter sandwich,
round cookies,
chocolate and chipped,
sweet bubbly pineapple juice
with a twisty silver cap—
and
a little note that says:
I LOVE YOU.
GUESS WHO?

Buzz

by Ann Rousseau Smith

Buzz . . .
Inside our classroom
Zooms a bee.
It zips, dips,
Tries to flee.

Buzz . . .
As students duck
And papers fly,
The whizzing bee
Comes racing by.

Buzz . . .

It zigzags back

Above the floor.

At last it finds

An open door.

Buzzzzzz . . .

Not Fair

by David L. Harrison

Sitting in school
On an April day
Isn't fair.
A guy should be flying
A kite with the wind
In his hair.

I know I'm supposed
To be doing my math,
I don't care.
Sitting in school
On an April day
Isn't fair.

Question

by Alice Schertle

Pencil stub, I must
ask myself: How many more
poems are in you?

The Eraser Poem

by Louis Phillips

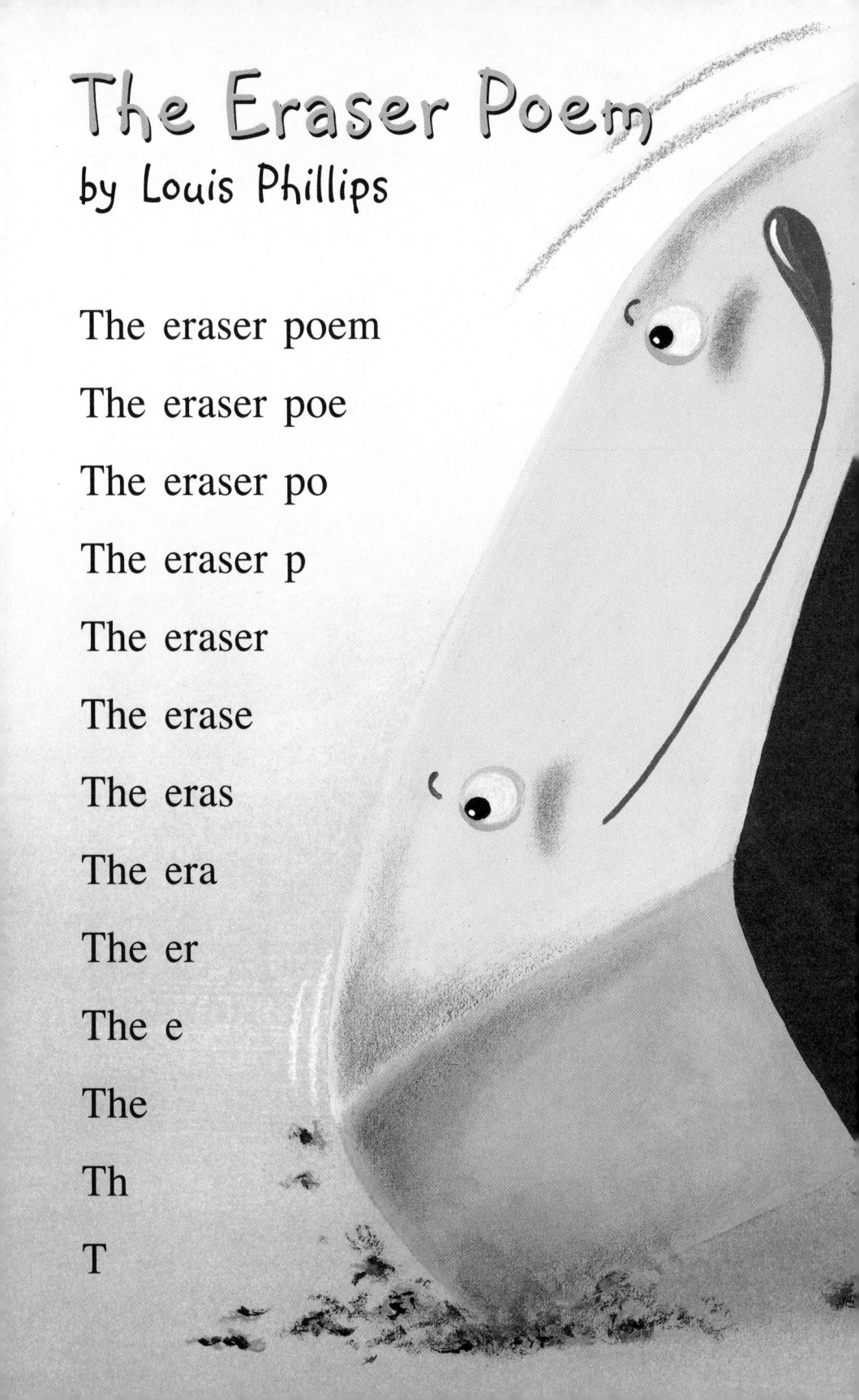

The eraser poem

The eraser poe

The eraser po

The eraser p

The eraser

The erase

The eras

The era

The er

The e

The

Th

T

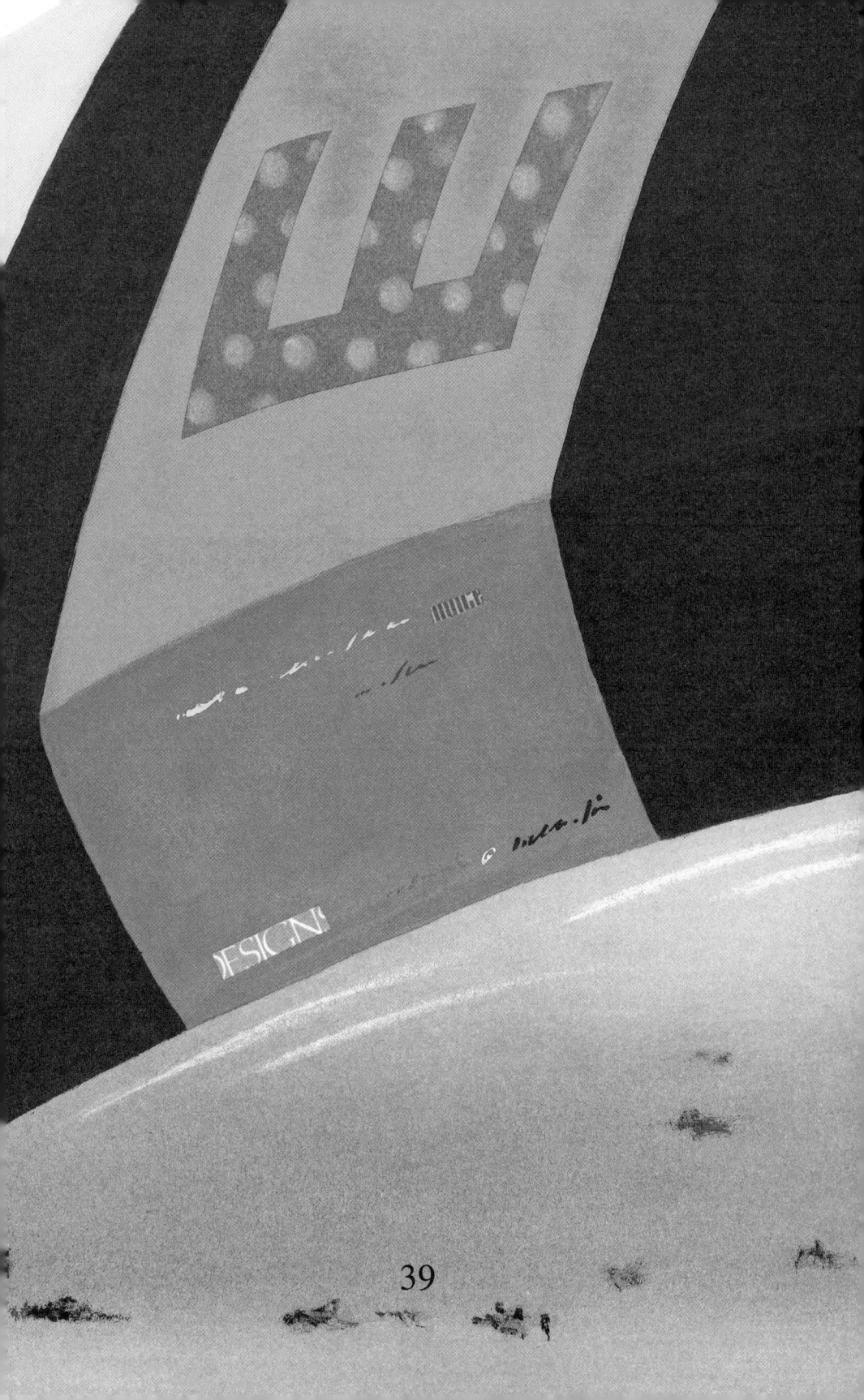
DESIGN

Measles

by Bruce Lansky

There are measles on my forehead.
There are measles on my nose.
There are measles on my elbows.
There are measles on my toes.

There are measles on the carpet.
There are measles on the chair.
There are measles on my glasses.
There are measles in my hair.

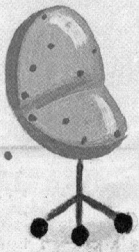

I'm so tired of painting measles.
I would like to take a rest.
I sure hope that I look sick enough
to miss tomorrow's test.

Spelling Bee

by Heidi Bee Roemer

Knees knocking.

Heart pounding.

I hear my teacher say,

"TARANTULA."

I spell the word.

I got it right!

Hip,

hip,

hip,

hooray!

his shot
his break in
Water

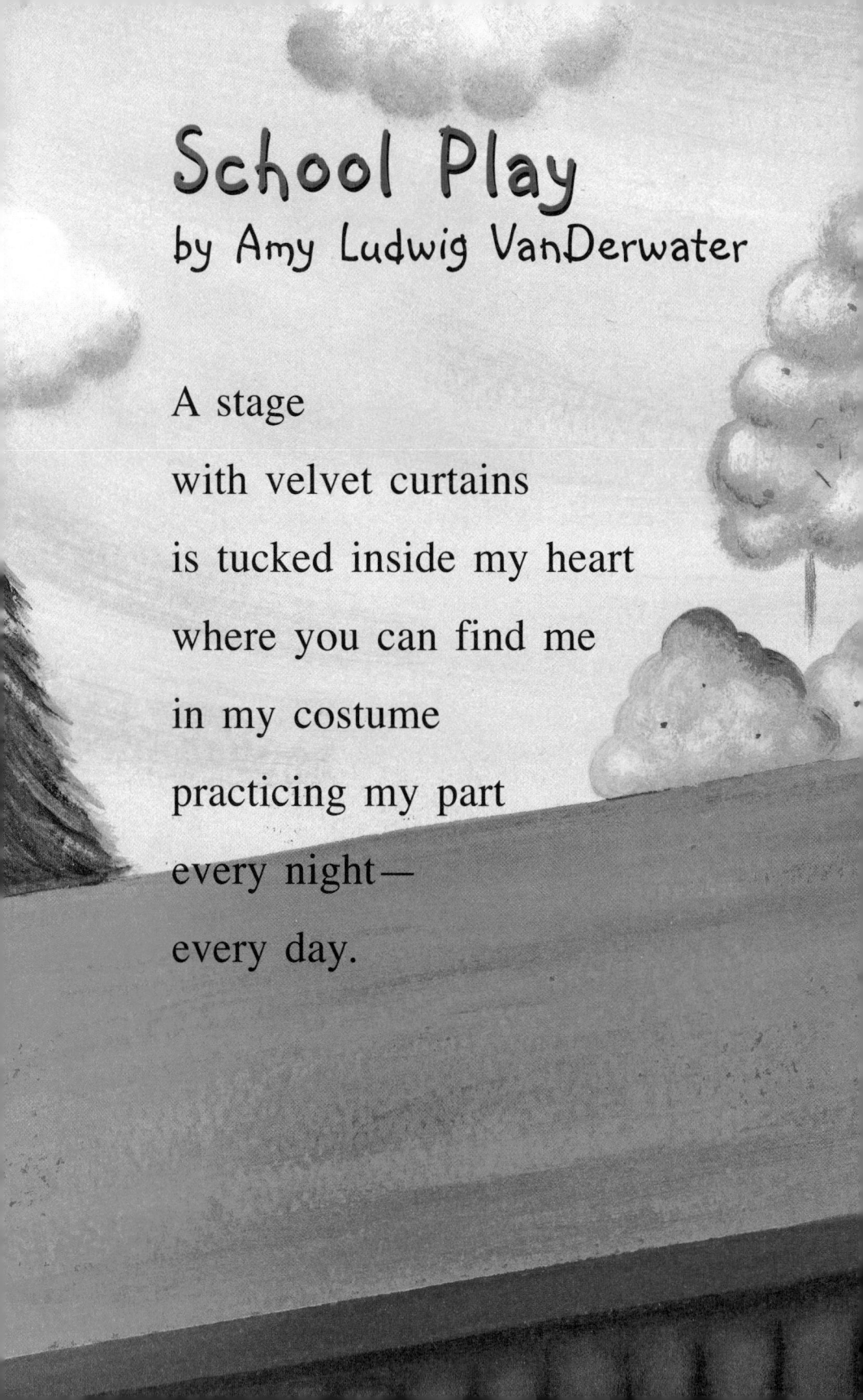

School Play

by Amy Ludwig VanDerwater

A stage
with velvet curtains
is tucked inside my heart
where you can find me
in my costume
practicing my part
every night—
every day.

I *will*
be ready
for our play.

Welcome

True Love

by Linda Kulp

Every day
after school
my cat sits
on the windowsill
waiting,
watching
for me
to come home
from school.
I open
the door
to her
purr-ing.

Index of Authors and Titles

Art Class, 24

Backpack Buddy, 14
Brüg, Sandra Gilbert, 28
Buzz, 32

Dotlich, Rebecca Kai, 8, 14

Eraser Poem, The, 38

Hamster Math, 10
Harrison, David L., 34
Hopkins, Lee Bennett, 16

Kotzas, Chetra, 30
Kulp, Linda, 46

Lansky, Bruce, 40
Lewis, J. Patrick, 12, 26
Library, 26
Listening, 28
Looking Through
the Microscope, 22
Lunch Bag, 30

Maps, 20
Measles, 40
My Teacher, 16

Not Fair, 34

Perkins, Leslie Danford, 24
Phillips, Louis, 38

Question, 36

Ready, 8
Roemer, Heidi Bee, 42

Schertle, Alice, 36
School Bus Driver, 12
School Play, 44
Settimo, Janet, 10
Show and Tell, 18
Spelling Bee, 42
Smith, Ann Rousseau, 32

True Love, 46

Upton, Elizabeth, 18

VanDerwater, Amy Ludwig, 44
Vargo, Sharon, 22

Yolen, Jane, 20